The Art of Outsourcing Information Technology

How Culture and Attitude Affect Client-Vendor Relationships

Dr. Jan D. Felton

authorHOUSE®

AuthorHouse™
1663 Liberty Drive, Suite 200
Bloomington, IN 47403
www.authorhouse.com
Phone: 1-800-839-8640

First published by AuthorHouse 6/4/2008

ISBN: 978-1-4343-6853-9 (sc)
ISBN: 978-1-4343-6852-2 (hc)

Library of Congress Control Number: 2008901911

Printed in the United States of America
Bloomington, Indiana

This book is printed on acid-free paper.

INTRODUCTION

Companies around the world are turning to outsourcing to help reduce or stabilize costs, access advanced technology, compensate for a lack of skilled information technology (IT) workers, and improve business efficiency. This quantitative and descriptive study investigated the impact of perceived differences in relationships, culture, and attitude between client and vendor employee groups on the success or failure of outsourcing IT in an organization. The survey sample consisted of 125 client employee participants and 125 vendor employee participants from two organizations in the United States. Chi-square analyses were used to assess the significant differences between the responses of the client employees and the vendor employees, and a content analysis was used to assess responses to open-ended questions. The results indicated that significant differences in culture appear to hinder the success of IT outsourcing and that a successful relationship between client and vendor is dependent upon recognition and comprehension of those cultural differences. The current research suggests that given the effects of globalization, a change process model is needed for identifying client and vendor strategic visions. This model takes an open systems perspective and relies on many organizational behavior concepts such as team dynamics, perceptions, and conflict management.

Dedication

This book is dedicated to my daughters, Rhonda Felton Bell, ReNita Michelle Felton and to my sister, Vermont Moore; brother, Wesley Diggs; and dear friend Maurice Claud, I know they will value the academic investment they can make that will benefit themselves and the people around them.

TABLE OF CONTENTS

LIST OF TABLES

CHAPTER 1:
INTRODUCTION

Information technology (IT) services outsourcing is the movement of IT activities of one corporation to another organization, sometimes to an entity in the United States and sometimes abroad (Marshall, 2003). Work is outsourced to achieve a variety of benefits: timely access to highly qualified technical talent, reduction of transit time to market, alleviation of cost pressures, speed of innovation, and deployment of existing IT resources to more strategic projects. Companies are increasingly outsourcing IT activities as a viable method for offsetting costs, and it has become a mainstream business practice in all industries. According to Rosencrance (2003), IBM signed a $600M, 7-year IT outsourcing deal with ING Technology Company in order to reduce costs. Marshall (2003) found that industries spent billions of dollars in labor-intensive back-office and IT costs which could have been outsourced more efficiently and economically. More companies are exploring ways to use outsourcing as a means of significantly reducing such costs.

Worldwide spending on IT outsourcing surpassed $68 billion in 2003 and is expected to top an annual $99 billion by 2007. Marshall (2003) further noted that in the United States, corporate and government spending on IT outsourcing services reached $30 billion in 2003 and was predicted to surpass $43 billion by 2007. Companies around the world are turning to outsourcing to help reduce or stabilize costs, access advanced technology, compensate for a lack of skilled IT workers, or improve business efficiency. According to the Gartner Research Group (2003), IT outsourcing among state and local governments was expected to grow at an annual rate of 25%, from more than $3 billion in 2002 to nearly $6 billion in 2005.

Lacity and Hirschheim (2000) explained that IT outsourcing involved transferring not just IT assets, leases, and staff, but also management responsibility for delivery of services, from internal IT functions to outside service vendors, though not necessarily to locations outside the country. It may be to remain competitive that many companies outsource work and projects, thus reducing costs, increasing productivity, and making optimal use of their available resources. The survival and growth of an organization may depend upon effective utilization of outsourcing information, which may deliver savings of nearly half the IT budget (Lacity & Hirschheim, 2000).

Companies are increasingly market driven and consequently assess their need for more advanced technology according to their estimate of what the market requires and justifies. The gap in companies' internal capabilities to invest properly in relationship management skills and processes may lead to failure on the vendor's part to meet the required level of expectation. The Dun & Bradstreet Barometer of Global Outsourcing (2000) concluded that between 20% and 25% of all outsourcing relationships broke down in any 2-year period and that as many as half were incapable of meeting the level of expectation within 5 years. Dun & Bradstreet further stated that nearly 70% of respondents reported that the reason for the failure of the relationship was that the supplier did not understand what was required.

According to the Meta Group (2003), in order for the client and vendor relationship to deliver value, the two sides' perceived economic impacts must be equitable synchronized: The magnitude of the client's expected value must be consistent with the vendor's expected, or achievable, value. In 1998, for example, vendors did not deliver 45% of IT outsourcing projects on time, and contractor abandoned 30% of the projects (Gartner Group, 2003). Previous studies indicated that outsourcing has been successful in many cases. On the other hand, as Soininen (1997) stated, the perception of the relationship between the client and the vendor (i.e., the application service provider) could affect the success or failure of IT outsourcing. According to an Everest Partners Group report (2003), in a good relationship, the client's expectations of how the objectives would be fulfilled are clearly defined and reasonable. This entails having a good understanding of their current environment in terms of service levels and the amount actually being spent to provide the service throughout the enterprise. The report also concluded that beyond the specifics of objectives and expectations, a good relationship also requires a suitable cultural mix in which both parties communicate effectively with each other.

A report by the Meta Group (2003) suggested that vendors should do a better job of communicating with clients and accommodating their issues and concerns. The report suggested that half of IT outsourcing projects would be considered unsuccessful in 2003 and 2004 because the service providers had not delivered the expected value. KPMG (1999) revealed that dissatisfaction with application service providers regarding client relationships resulted in more than 70% of clients planning not to renew their existing contract. Research investigation by Cole-Gomolski (1998) indicated that more than half of the outsourcing clients believed the quality of their vendors' service had declined in 1998.

In essence, cultural awareness and cultural self awareness involve the following:

1. Self knowledge to anticipate how one's own behaviors are affected by culture.

2. An understanding of how one's "buttons are pushed" and how clients from different cultures may push these buttons because of their different cultural value systems. For example, many healthcare professionals have been socialized in Western worldviews regarding time. However, a client from another culture may have completely different notions about time and be constantly late for sessions. The professional may become frustrated and view the client's behavior as resistance when in fact it is simply cultural difference.

3. An appreciation of the dynamics of cultural differences. When service providers and clients come from different cultural backgrounds, inevitably there will be miscommunication. Cultural awareness involves knowing what can go wrong in cross-cultural communications and how to set it right (Gartner).

Many vendors put call center employees through accent training. However, cultural differences go much deeper than accent. They include variations in religion, modes of dress, social activities, and even the way a question is answered. According to the Gartner Group (2003), by 2004, more than 80% of all U.S. companies will have considered shifting domestic IT jobs overseas, whereas 40% of all U.S. organizations will have completed some type of pilot scheme or will have actually outsourced IT services to service providers outside of the United States. Today, many organizations may not be comfortable about outsourcing, but with the increasing emphasis on acquiring the most recent and innovative technology to address growing competition, it may be the solution of necessity.

Problem Statement

The reasons for outsourcing, and its increasing popularity, have been broken down into two critical values provided to firms: significantly reduced cost (estimates vary from 25% to 65%, depending on the complexity of the project and the length of time the firms have worked together), and reduced time to market seen when existing capabilities can be extended (Gartner Research Group, 2004). The Gartner Group indicated that between 20% and 25% of IT outsourcing projects are not delivered on time or are abandoned by the vendor. There is a possibility that communication between the parties to an outsourcing agreement may be a significant factor in its success or failure. In an age when reduced time to market and collaborative development are key factors in maintaining a profit margin, inadequate communication can become a barrier. If communications are infrequent between the client and vendor, and if progress is not communicated well, requirements can be misunderstood, or a project may not be completed to the client's expectation. Effective communication ensures that the vendor understands the deliverables.

Background of the Problem

Increasing numbers of businesses and IT firms are outsourcing their software and Web development tasks. Gartner (2004) has estimated that currently half of the Fortune 500 companies have utilized outsourcing for their development needs and estimates that by the end of 2004, 40% of U.S. companies will either develop, test, support, or store software overseas, with another 40% considering doing the same (Gartner). Several industries, from computer software to telemarketing, have begun aggressively shifting white-collar work out of the United States. The United States currently accounts for more than half of worldwide spending on IT outsourcing, with a growing portion of this spending going to countries such as India, Russia, and the Philippines, and according to Dun & Bradstreet (2000), this trend will continue. Forrester Research (2003) predicted that beginning in calendar year 2003, companies would move 3.3 million U.S. services industry jobs and $136 billion in wages out of the country over the following 15 years.

Many organizations are failing to manage outsourcing transitions in a way that delivers a satisfactory outcome. According to a recent Dataquest study (2003), 53% of all outsourcing clients reported having renegotiated a contract, and in nearly one quarter of these renegotiations, the original service provider lost the account. According to the literature, the existing structures and internal relationships may contribute to a lot of difficulties and tensions between vendor and client (Willcocks, Lacity, & Fitzgerald, 1995). Managing and meeting client expectations in outsourcing is a major challenge in IT-enabled outsourcing services, where the nature of the services themselves and the rapid changes in technology and tools introduce an additional level of complexity.

All companies have a culture, but no two companies are the same. Dun & Bradstreet (2000) suggested that an organization establish precise, measurable objectives, document expected improvements for core business as a result of outsourcing, create a scorecard that quantifies each objective, and implement a regular review process with internal personnel and representatives of the outsourcing vendor. Although every firm seeks more efficient and more cost-effective strategies, some companies ignore the potential problems that may accompany outsourcing.

Research has indicated that the primary problem is language because of idiomatic expressions and subtle cultural nuances associated with the use of particular words. Thus communication frequently breaks down when dealing with overseas companies. The client and vendor firms are assured that the staff and project managers can speak English. In most cases, the staff actually only read English and have inadequate speaking or translation skills. Meta Group (2004) gave a representative example: Although English is one of the official languages in India, pronunciation and accents can vary tremendously even within the country. Many countries do not promote English as a common language for communication; therefore, difficulties might arise in communicating a company's requirements and having projects successfully executed.

A vendor may fail to deliver a project at the time expected by the client, for example. When this occurs, the barrier may not be that the project is late, but that it was caused by something as seemingly obvious as a 12-hour time zone difference. This is the sort of thing that must be understood at the outset of the contract to avoid frustration on both sides. Adaptations for time must be established to facilitate regular communication. Another barrier could be the loss of in-house knowledge about the relationship of the business and IT operations. There may be a loss of information about dependencies and why certain IT functions operate in a particular manner in international outsourcing. This can easily occur with personnel changes and inadequate records of circumstances unique to the vendor or client.

International outsourcing involves complexity and risks not found in a typical domestic outsourcing (Everest Partners Group,

2005). These risks are cultural, political, financial, technological, managerial, and legal. One example is whether existing warranties will transfer to the supplier. When considering application outsourcing, management must be very clear with respect to its expectations. The allure of outsourcing as a way to address company inefficiencies, or budgetary concerns may blind management to the potential dangers of shifting an internal process to outside contractors. One of the first risks to consider is the possible tension between client and vendor employees arising out of different institutional relationships, attitudes, and cultures (Lacity & Hirschheim, 2000).

Problems will not be solved if the two sides cannot talk to each other with understanding (Snow, 1959). Different cultures and cultural backgrounds bring obstacles, challenges, and difficulties. When an outsourcing relationship starts, there is a great deal companies have to learn from each other. An organization's culture can be understood as the sum of the assumptions, beliefs, and values that its members share and is expressed through what is done, how it is done, and who is doing it (Farmer, 1990). Farmer further stated that until external forces put it to the test, the culture of an organization is often taken for granted by its members; its impact on decisions, behaviors, and communication are inadequately evaluated, and its symbolic and structural boundaries poorly considered.

Outsourcing has become a major trend in areas such as IT. In some cases, the entire IT department of a company is outsourced, including planning and business process as well as the installation, management, and servicing of network and workstations. Outsourcing can range from a large major contract in which a company like IBM manages IT services for a company like Xerox, to the practice of hiring contractors and temporary office workers on an individual basis (Kakabadse, N., & Kakabadse, A., 2000). The relationship between the client and provider is different from what it has been historically, and the providers chosen by clients for outsourcing of their functions are being chosen in a much more technical manner.

Purpose of the Study

The purpose of this descriptive study was twofold.

1. To determine if culture and attitudes affect client-vendor relationships.

2. To determine if the client and the vendor should be working together as a team and, to some extent, blending two companies.

3. To determine which issues more significantly affect a decline in new business and vendor productivity and client satisfaction levels.

Nature of the Study

According to Sproull (1995), research questions can be used to make inferences about populations through the use of samples. This quantitative, descriptive research study collected data through the administration of a survey questionnaire. The study was limited to information supplied by survey respondents. The descriptive study was nonexperimental and nonquantitative. The survey was designed to answer, in particular, the following questions:

1. What do the data obtained from the administration of a survey questionnaire indicate as to client and vendor employees' respective perceptions of each other's attitudes and cultural values where the outsourcing of technology is concerned?

2. Are there significant differences among client and vendor groups in their respective perceptions of each other's attitudes and

cultural values that may affect successful outsourcing of technology by reducing vendor productivity and client satisfaction?

The relevant perceptions were examined by means of a descriptive research design that consists of two or more defined concepts as variables, as related to a conceptual framework, survey instrument, and determined relationships or associations among the variables. The data were subjected to descriptive analysis, as well as chi-square and content analysis. Content analysis was used with the open-ended questions to identify any further perceptions reported by the client and vendor subjects regarding each other's organizational values and culture. This methodology is described in greater detail in chapter 3.

Significance of the Study

The significance of this study was the need to substantiate the importance of differences between client and vendor employees' respective perceptions of the other's organizational values and cultures within IT, particularly since, between 20% and 25% of all outsourcing relationships fail in any 2-year period and half predictably fail within 5 years (Dun & Bradstreet, 2000). Dun & Bradstreet further stated that nearly 70% of respondents reported that a relationship fails because the supplier does not understand what they are supposed to do, reinforcing the concept that in large part failure is as a result of incomplete communication or miscommunication. It is an issue that will become more significant as more organizations turn to outsourcing, with a total forecast annual value of more than $200 billion worldwide (Marshall, 2003).

Clients and vendors approach outsourcing with different philosophies, but they rarely discuss those philosophies and the impact they may have on the relationship. Language or cultural problems might contribute to the dissatisfactions of clients. There is also a pervasive attitude that because the work is outsourced, the relationship does not need to be cultivated or managed and that it can simply be allowed to happen as one element in an automated process. As a result, clients and vendors may be ill prepared to ensure that their relationship is mutually driven toward achievement of the intended and agreed-upon results (Marshall, 2003).

Earl (1996) and Hoffman and Klepper (2000) observed that organizational culture is relevant to outsourcing success and that the relationship between client and vendor culture contributes to success or failure in outsourcing technology. Therefore, the emphasis in this study was laid upon determining if there were significant differences between client and vendor cultures as well as between their respective employees' perceptions of each other's organizational values and culture within the outsourcing IT department.

Corporate culture is the total of the values, virtues, accepted behaviors, and political environment of an organization. According to Meta Group (2004), during 2004-2005, outsourcing will divide into commodity and transformational services. Infrastructure services will mirror grid-computing structures and develop consumption-based pricing. Through 2006-2007, transformational services (e.g., application development maintenance and business process outsourcing) will divide between horizontal (function commonality) and vertical (specialized) business process/services outsourcing functions.

IT has been further examined in the works of numerous researchers, including Antonucci and Tucker (1998), Barrett (1996), Earl (1996), and Graham and Scarborough (1997), with a view to identifying the reasons various companies are choosing to outsource their IT operations. These include, but are not limited to:

1. Reducing or controlling operating costs.
2. Making capital funds available for other purposes,.
3. Obtaining access to highly trained and skilled specialists.
4. Improving business or company focus.
5. Improving service quality.
6. Accelerating reengineering benefits.
7. Focusing on core competencies.

The dimensions and the related perceived benefits of outsourcing have grown dramatically. A survey of over 1,200 companies reveals why managers like both long term and short-term outsourcing contracts (Halvey & Melby, 1996). The top five short-term pros include, but are not limited to:

1. Lower operating costs. Access to the outside providers' lower cost structure is one of the most compelling short-term benefits of outsourcing. In a recent Outsourcing Institute survey, companies reported that on average, they saw a 9% reduction in costs through outsourcing.

2. More capital funds. Outsourcing reduces the need to invest capital in noncore business functions, thereby making capital funds more available for core areas. Outsourcing also can improve corporate financial measurements by eliminating the need to show return on equity from capital investments in noncore areas.

3. A cash infusion. Outsourcing can involve the transfer of assets from the client to the provider. Equipment, facilities, vehicles and licenses used in current operations all have a value and are, in effect, sold to the provider as of the transaction, resulting in a cash payment to the client.

4.   Access to new resources. Companies may outsource because they do not have access to the required resources within. For example, if an organization would like to expand its operations, especially into a new geographic area, outsourcing is a viable and important alternative to building the needed capability from the ground up, and

5.   Better overall IT management. Outsourcing is certainly one option for managing an out-of-control IT function.

Worldwide spending on IT outsourcing surpassed $68 billion in 2002 and is expected to top $99 billon by 2007 (Drucker, 1995). Drucker also stated that by 2010, organizations would be outsourcing all functions that were support rather than revenue producing in order to lower their overall operating costs and improve service delivery. As Cole-Gomolski (1996) noted, more than half of outsourcing clients at the time believed that the quality of their vendors' services had declined in the previous year.

The strategic factors that drive organizations to outsource are those that have a direct impact on a company's overall marketplace position. They include corporate reengineering to focus on core business functions: to increase employee and management demands for service, to increase compliance with regulatory requirements of organizations operating across geographical boundaries, to access the best services, to spread risks, and to cope with increasing cost pressures. The current trends in IT outsourcing will likely continue to evolve as IT outsourcing continues to be seen as a way to improve a company's bottom line. In the near future, there will likely be new reasons why companies are looking to outsource, new types of outsourcing relationships, and new reasons why certain providers are chosen. However, one thing will remain the same: every business will do anything to get an edge over the competition (Hoffman & Klepper, 2000).

In the past, outsourcing was only done on short-term contracts, but this is no longer the case. In fact, the results of the Oxford Executive Research Briefings included the finding that even 8 years ago, 48% of all outsourcing contracts were at least four years long (as cited in Hoffman & Klepper, 2000). Not only are the lengths of outsourcing relationships increasing but the types of relationship and of company culture also are changing. One of the basic premises of outsourcing IT is that the vendor can provide the same services to the client at a lower cost and still make a profit.

An organization specializing in IT can offer two major benefits: the economies of scale associated with large operations may reduce computing costs; and the provision of specialized experience, of greater cultural diversity, and of sheer expertise may offer increased efficiency and effectiveness (Cronk & Sharp, 1999). If this is true, the results of this study may contribute to the understanding on the part of managers concerning the effects of relationships, lack of communication, and service issues associated with improving the company's bottom line that could lead to a more meaningful business objective.

Theoretical Framework

One of the best-known theories relating to organizational culture and helping to explain its influences on particular organizations is Schein's (2001) model. According to Schein, elements of organizational culture may include:

1. Stated and unstated values.
2. Overt and implicit expectations of members' behavior.

3. Customs and rituals.

4. Organizational climate (i.e., the feelings evoked by the ways members interact with one another, with outsiders, and with their environment).

Schein's (2001) organization cultural model entailed reinterpreting conflicts as products of different sets of experiences. Rather than starting from an assumption that something was right or wrong, an approach using the organizational culture model would begin from the standpoint that subcultures examine the assumptions underlying the behavior of the client and vendor, honor the experiences that led to those assumptions, and then investigate whether those assumptions still worked well (Schein). Morgan's (1997) organizational model identified three essential strengths of such a model as a method to assess human system:

1. It made clear the importance of creating appropriate systems of shared meaning to help people work together toward desired outcomes.

2. It required members, especially leaders, to acknowledge the impact of their behavior on the organization's culture.

3. It encouraged the view that the perceived relationship between an organization and its environment was affected by the organization's basic assumptions.

Schein's (2001) and Morgan's (1997) models may be applied to an understanding of the effects of cultural differences between client and vendor on a transitional path to the outsourcing of technology. Both models were predicated on the importance of creating appropriate systems of shared meaning to help people work together toward desired outcomes. They required members, especially leaders, to acknowledge the impact of their behavior on the organization's culture (Schein). According to Schein, the bottom line for leaders was that if they did not become conscious of the cultures in which they were embedded, those cultures would manage them.

The theoretical framework of this study was based on the organizational cultural model suggested by Cash and Konsynski (1994). This model consisted of three variables: technology, people, and business processes. The model depicted variable relationships within an organization and provided a framework for overall organizational design that may establish and enhance the client-vendor relationship. Schein's (2001) and Morgan's (1997) models, too, were helpful in understanding the linkage between organizational cultural and IT outsourcing.

Schein's (2001) and Morgan's (1997) models stress that an organization should examine the assumptions underlying the behavior of the client and vendor. The model developed by Cash and Konsynski points out that the variable relationships within an organization should provide a framework for designing technology, people, and business processes for a more successful organization. The model also indicated a further need to improve management relationships with the vendor in order to make better business decisions.

Managing the overall relationship is the area where the greatest effort is required (Cash & Konsynski 1994). Cash and Konsynski suggested that the client and vendor should work collaboratively and effectively as a team. The Cash and Konsynski model points out that it is important to take the cultures of the two organizations into consideration when structuring and defining business processes and that the client and vendor should agree in advance on the communication channels and responsibilities to ensure success.

Scope of the Study

A descriptive design was used in order to examine the perceptions of the understanding of attitudes and cultural differences among client and vendor groups. The design consisted of two or more defined concepts as variables, as related to a conceptual framework, survey instrument, and determined relationships or associations among the variables. This descriptive research study set out to investigate the perceptions held by the employees of a U.S. federal agency (the client) and the employees of a U.S. company (the vendor), respectively, regarding each other's organizational values and culture within the IT department. It also sought to establish an IT outsourcing model that focused on shared practices, with the aim of increasing success rates in outsourcing technology. To be culturally sensitive and competent, it is necessary to develop an awareness of the ways cultures differ, how these differences affect interactions with clients, and how the client perceives the interaction (Cash, 1994).

This researcher's use of the survey method employed the positivist and behavioral methodological approaches. Positivism implies that research is deductive through questioning. According to Anderson (1983), this approach begins from the standpoint that knowledge is derived from an objective interpretation of assumptions, without any of the subjective biases or a priori knowledge of the scientist coming into play. In Anderson's view, this approach should aim to advance the researcher's understanding of the ways in which differing information technologies tend to divide cultures and of the significance of communication between client and vendor.

Limitations

This descriptive study set out to determine if there are differences between client and vendor employees in their respective perceptions of each other's organizational values and culture within the outsourcing IT department. The samples selected for the survey data collection were representative of the population from which they were chosen. The researcher expected 250 survey questionnaires to be returned that would provide data for analysis and interpretation, permitting the subsequent formulation of conclusions and recommendations.

The conclusions were limited, first, by the range of information and data available to this researcher from books, documents, reports, journal articles, and various database searches. As Babbie (1998) and Rea and Parker (1997) pointed out, where any study is concerned, there could be unknown research and documentation not taken into consideration, the absence of which could significantly influence results. However, this is true of any research investigation, regardless of the sample population used or the method employed.

The volume of data collected from administration of the survey may also have limited the conclusions. All participants were anonymous. It was important to offer anonymity as an incentive to participate, because the greater the number of people involved in the study, the more compelling the findings, as is true of any study or research project, whatever the design (Leedy, 1997; Rea & Parker, 1997). Babbie (1998) suggested that limitations might be evidenced in the statistical analysis. In his view, uncontrolled variables often limited the applicability and generalizability of a study. Some of these, however, are inherent in the research situation and the investigator has limited control over them.

Delimitations

Because of time and scale limitations, the client and vendor participants included in the descriptive research study were selected only from one client agency and one corresponding vendor company. Different findings may have been obtained if the survey had been administered to a different population.

Definitions of Terms

The researcher took the definitions from various sources, including those consulted for the literature review, business glossaries, and Internet sources, as cited where applicable in this research report. The following terms and acronyms are central to the study:

Outsourcing: The term is generally defined as contracting with outside vendors to do various IT functions such as data entry, data center operations, application maintenance and development, disaster recovery, and network management and operations. Vendors may be individual IS/IT professionals, consulting firms, employee leasing companies, full-service providers (Antonucci & Lordi, 1998).

Application Service Provider (ASP): A company that manages and delivers application capabilities to multiple entities from data centers across a wide area network (WAN). It is based on delivering software as a service rather than a product priced according to a license fee and maintenance contract set by a vendor (Davies, 2002).

Content Analysis: A research technique that is used to describe the objective, systematically analyze the content of written, spoken and quantitative description of manifest content of communications. It is a research tool that is focused on the actual content and internal features of media. Content analysis can provides valuable historical/

cultural insights over time through analysis of texts (Berelson, 1974).

Contracting Relationships: A contracting relationship can be viewed as a range or continuum. At one extreme are market-like relationships in which the organization has a choice of many vendors capable of performing the work, relatively short contract durations, and the ability to switch to another vendor at the end of a contract for future work of the same type without additional cost or inconvenience (Jones, 1997). At the other extreme are long-term partnerships, arrangements in which the organization contracts repeatedly with the same vendor and develops a mutually beneficial relationship that lasts a long time. The middle of the continuum is occupied by relationships that must endure and remain reasonably harmonious until a major piece of work is completed; these are termed intermediate relationships (Jones).

Corporate Culture: Culture consists of the shared norms, values, and practices associated with a nation, organization, or profession (Hofstede, 1980). Corporate culture, then, is the sum of the values, virtues, accepted behaviors, and political environment of an organization (Bliss, 1999). An organization's culture is composed of values, behaviors, and attitudes (Hatch & Schulz, 2001). It provides continuity, structure, common meaning, and order, giving rise to stable patterns of interaction within the organization.

IT Infrastructure: IT includes the technology, design, development, installation, and implementation of information systems and applications. IT infrastructure, thus, refers to the complex set of IT resources that provides the technological foundation for a firm's present and future business applications (Duncan, 1995a, 1995b). The technology usually includes platform hardware and software, network and telecommunications technology, core organizational data, and data processing applications fundamental to the business (Duncan). It is frequently complex, both in technological characteristics and in its history of evolution. The characteristics of the infrastructure determine the feasibility of changes and innovations in business applications (Jones, 1997).

IT Outsourcing: IT outsourcing is the process of turning over part or all of an organization's IT functions to external service providers; it may involve purchasing information systems equipment or services from a vendor external to the firm. The aim is to achieve economic, technological, and strategic benefits. To better achieve effectiveness in IT outsourcing for both the vendor and the client parties, both may need to adopt mutual strategies for the delivery of IT functions (Jacobides, 1998; King, J. & Cole-Gomolski, 1999; King, W., & Malhotra, 2000). The term may also apply to the use of outside resources to perform noncore functions (Huber, 1993).

International Outsourcing: International outsourcing occurs where a customer turns over responsibility for a function performed in more than one country. For example, a customer might turn over work being done in the United States, the United Kingdom, and France to a service provider who would then perform the work in the United States, the United Kingdom, and France using its related companies in those countries (Everest Partners Group, 2005).

Service provider or *vendor:* These terms refer to the organization providing the outsourced service. Synonymous terms are "outsourcer" or "supplier" (Khosrowpour, 1995; Khosrowpour, Subramanian, Gunderman, & Saber (1996)).

Summary

Chapter 1 introduced the investigation and was based on the initial section of the study. It also set out the problem statement, the nature of the study, the research questions, and the purpose of the study, its theoretical framework, definitions of technical terms, and the limitations, scope, and significance of the study.

Chapter 2 presents an in-depth review of the literature relevant to the research study and its most important variables. Specifically, IT outsourcing literature was reviewed as it pertained to the differences between client and vendor employees in their respective perceptions of each other's organizational values and culture as they relate to the success or failure of IT outsourcing within an organization. Accordingly, the chapter considers scholarly perspectives and controversies relevant to client and vendor cultures.

The current trends in IT outsourcing will likely continue to evolve as this process continues to be seen as a way to improve a company's profits, so that there was a clear need for a study, or studies, of this kind.

CHAPTER 2:
LITERATURE REVIEW

This chapter reviews the literature pertinent to the client-vendor relationship and to the culture and attitudes that may affect an organization's success or potential problems in outsourcing IT services. Hoffman and Klepper (2000) suggested that managers should understand organizational culture in terms of sociability and solidarity so they can effectively deal with potential problems in the new technology assimilation. The chapter is divided into five sections: (a) an examination of the literature on outsourcing relationship practices, (b) outsourcing framework and strategies, (c) client and vendor culture, (d) investigative methodology, and (e) a summary of the works consulted and their relationship to the study.

The primary strategy used to access the literature was to search online databases such as ProQuest, MasterFile Premier, CQ Researcher, CQ Weekly, and Gale Virtual Reference Library for relevant information. These led to articles in professional journals marked by such key words as *IT, information technology, information systems, data management, outsourcing, vendor technology,* and *consulting.* The issues and concerns identified in the review were also used to create a survey instrument designed to answer the research questions.

Outsourcing Relationships

To minimize conflicts and problems within a partnership between client and vendor, King and Malhotra (2000) suggest that it is important for the organizations to establish a common goal even when different corporate goals are complementary and evolving constantly. Pinnington and Woolcock (1997) argued that the key to a successful outsourcing relationship is to establish internal processes that support the relationship, to establish metrics, and to define expectations that client and vendor can agree on in advance.

Managing the overall relationship is the area where the greatest effort is required, because it is here that problems are most likely to occur. Relationship management addresses areas beyond the provision of products and services and deals with elements of compatibility, which are often overlooked as nonessential (i.e., not relating to products, services, or pricing), yet are often the source of client dissatisfaction (Fee, 2001) A successful relationship between client and vendor requires ongoing assessment and fine tuning, setting, and validating mutual goals. This process entails agreeing upon and analyzing metrics for better decision making, setting up incentives for client success, establishing continuing trust by demonstrating flexibility, and honoring commitments (2001).

Having established metrics also provides the client and vendor with a benchmark to measure against (Pinnington & Woolcock, 1997). Clients' expectations may be too high, and their confidence in IT outsourcing excessive, so they may engage in unrealistically long term contracts with service providers and then suffer losses when unpredicted changes arise. Such contracts fail to make allowance for a vendor's failure to fulfill client expectations and may result in a loss of opportunity to seek better and more economical outsourcing alternatives (1997).

Companies should rely on outsourcing relationships to give them a competitive advantage in the marketplace, yet more than 25% of all outsourcing relationships failed in the initial 2-year period (Dun & Bradstreet, 2003). Outsourcing relationships differ from other commercial relationships (Benko, 1992, 1993; Jones, 1997). First, the outsourcing relationship is generally of a long-term nature--roughly 3 or more years (Kruger, 2000). Second, the parties involved usually work together closely throughout the term of the relationship. Third, the project task cannot be easily defined and is usually subject to change (Kakabadse, N., & Kakabadse, A. 2000; Lacity & Hirschheim, 1993).

Regardless of the particulars of a contract, any relationship of this nature will only succeed if all the parties get from the relationship what they expect (Klepper, 1995). It is accordingly necessary that each party should be aware of the other party's expectations. Klepper suggested that individuals responsible for managing the outsourcing relationship for the client should receive specific training on how to complete the assignment successfully. This would entail gaining a thorough knowledge of the business goals of the contract and of the specific performance criteria agreed to and a clear view of each individual's roles and responsibilities, chains of authority, and reporting structures. The same information should be communicated to the larger end-user community. In this way, the entire organization understands what is intended and expected, how problems will be identified and resolved, what will be the communication channels and other process elements. This training and communication may help counter resentment or resistance even before it arises (Klepper).

The client should provide in the contract for a formal relationship management structure linking the client and vendor (Jones, 1997). This process could involve the forming of joint management teams that would have responsibility for day-to-day, tactical, and strategic aspects of the relationship. The Gartner Group (2003) recommends that, if possible, the client and vendor should meet to establish a relationship. If this cannot be done, then at least there should be a substitute such as a video of the provider's facility along with personal commentary by the principal employees.

Marshall (2003) stated that in spite of reported problems, more than 30% of the organizations that had already outsourced one business process were actively searching for additional outsourcing opportunities in other areas. The Dataquest 1999-2004 market forecast for business process outsourcing was that the BPO market was experiencing and was expected to continue to experience record growth in the United States and abroad. The report noted that, worldwide, BPO services were expected to grow from $207.7 billion in 1999 to $543.5 billion in 2004, a compounded annual growth rate of 21.2%.

The backlash in the United States over outsourcing is not really deserved, according to an IT trade organization that claims the positives far outweigh the negatives (Gartner Group, 2003). As demand for offshore IT outsourcing services grows in the coming years, companies will be faced with the problem of limited outsourcing resources in more established markets for IT services, such as India, Ireland, and the Philippines. China currently has 200,000 IT professionals involved in the software export industry, with an additional 50,000 entering the workforce each year. Gartner Group further stated that even though most Chinese IT service employees have strong technical skills, they lack proficiency in spoken and written English and have little knowledge of Western culture (Gartner).

The first step to take before executing an international outsourcing successfully is to decide how the contracting will be done (Everest Partners Group, 2005). Contracting can be done in a core country under that country's laws, but with global application. Contracting can also be done simultaneously in various countries, which require little coordination but lose many of the advantages of a global outsourcing. A third alternative, combining benefits of both the centralized and decentralized approach, is to develop a core contract in a core country, and then replicate that agreement, with appropriate localizations, in the other countries. A key factor in deciding on the contracting approach is the motivation for an international outsourcing transaction, the relationship between the client and vendor, and the decentralized approach works. Each country team should include people with expertise in the outsourced function, finance, operations, law, tax, labor/employment, and outsourcing contracting (2005).

The organizational structure, as represented by its managers, is specifically responsible for ensuring that everyone understands the objectives and is comfortable with the tasks and relationships involved (Schmidt & Judiesch, 1990). This process should include identifying the problems, brainstorming solutions, and setting the path to achieve desired business results.

Effective organizational structure can help to avoid undesired outcomes. As the IT industry matures, it becomes increasingly relevant to look at its relationship to the principles of the client and vendor. IT outsourcing relationships may risk failure if they lack focus on the human aspect (Dewett & Jones, 2001).

Outsourcing Framework and Strategies

Frameworks and strategies for achieving successful outsourcing outcomes are presented by such researchers as Cheon, Grover, and Teng (1995); Kini (1996); Lacity and Hirschheim (1993); Loh and Venkatraman (1992); Ruber (1995), and Yesulatitis (1997). Frameworks include identifying organizational needs, implementing them, and finding outsourcing partners. Strategies include developing time line measurements and responsiveness, maintaining control over the project, and defining the outsourcing agreement.

Successes and failures in outsourcing are assessed according to the satisfaction of end users (Antonucci & Tucker, 1998; Asbrand 1997a, 1997b; Benko, 1993; Guterl, 1996; Mullin, 1996; Pinnington & Woolcock, 1997). They specified the following areas to review:

1. The identification of objectives.
2. The measurement of vendor and client satisfaction.
3. The addressing of cultural differences.
4. The understanding of requirements.

The organization usually defines its business strategies first and then its IT requirements (Feurer, Chaharbaghi, Weber, & Wargin, 2000). Other technologies are then aligned. This sequential approach defines strategies, processes, and actions in relation to the technologies available. However, the technologies that drive the critical success factors of an organization are not identified in such approaches. Clearly, a much better line of attack, therefore, is one in which strategies; actions, processes, and technologies are defined and aligned concurrently. The aim of such an approach is to present a business alignment approach that enables the integration of new business processes with new generations of information systems (2000.).

Outsourcing a business process or function requires a partnership arrangement between client and vendor (Barnsley, 1997). It involves a sharing of risks and rewards and often follows an open-book approach where client and vendor agree to share information regarding operating costs, revenues, actual service levels, and other sensitive information. As organizational change takes place through the course of an outsourcing engagement, the foundation is thereby laid for greater productivity and innovation and better results (1997).

Managers must also be proactive and oversee the mechanism designed to ensure that the outsourcing provider operates in a performance zone consonant with the organization's objectives. Organizations should, in fact, develop outsourcing metrics and key performance-monitoring parameters that may be built into the outsourcing agreement and be subject to an ongoing assessment (Earl, 1996).

Client and Vendor Culture

Organizations have become increasingly global (Edberg, Grupe, & Kuechler, 2001). IT managers have realized that their strategies need to support a global rather than a local market. One of the most obvious issues in global IT management is that of culture. According to the Gartner Group (2003), it is important to take the cultures of the two organizations into consideration when structuring the relationship and defining work guidelines. The client and the vendor should agree in advance on the communication channels, escalation processes, responsibilities, and authorities to ensure success. When choosing an outsourcing vendor, the chances of a successful engagement will be greater if each competing company has a culture compatible with that of the client (Gartner, 2003).

Guptill (2002) stated that if the cultural and communications fit was wrong, or if support strategies differed, or if sales teams competed for the same clients, revenues and relationships would suffer. Cultural compatibility is a vital component in selecting the correct partner (Barnsley, 1997). Barnsley also suggested that the client-vendor must have the same objectives and be heading in the same direction; for example, both parties should be able to agree that the task can be precisely specified, that the means of achieving the outcome and performance can be accurately evaluated, and that there are satisfactory means of resolving conflicts (1997).

Organizational culture is often underestimated or overlooked as a factor with an impact on the initial success or failure of the introduction of some new technology into an organization (Hoffman & Klepper, 2000). Hoffman and Klepper also suggested that managers should understand organizational culture in terms of sociability and solidarity so they can effectively deal with potential problems in the new technology assimilation. According to Edberg et al. (2001), One of the most obvious issues in global IT management is that of language. Should English be used throughout an organization, or should native languages be used in the different branches of organizations in various countries? Should English be used as the main language in organizations? The language issue raises these questions and others. In a similar manner, different countries may have different laws, currencies, time zones, cultures, and terminology. Although IT is essential to the success of a business, the personalities, culture, and management style within the IT section of an organization are likely to be considerably different from those same elements in other units of the business (2001).

Sabherwal (1999) suggested that culture is an important element in the interpersonal and inter-organizational relationships between clients and vendors. In many cases of IT outsourcing, projects require the vendor to send experienced staff to the client company, and the client to send management staff to the vendor company. With the development of vast amounts of networks and relationships between the client and vendor companies in a highly tense environment with time constraints, there are inevitably problems associated within the relationship and trust-building process.

Fee (2001) asserted that the client needs to be properly informed. A client management staff poorly informed about the implementation process may set unreasonable time constraints on projects, resulting in work overloads and stress for developers. Previous studies indicated that even though outsourcing had been successful in many cases, the nature of the relationship and the effectiveness of the intercommunication between client and vendor could substantially determine the success or failure of an IT outsourcing operation (Soininen, 1997).

Lacity, Hirschheim, and Willcocks (1994) studied the reasons outsourcing deals often failed to produce the anticipated results, noting that many outsourcing deals were undertaken based upon the vendor's proclaimed ability to provide outstanding reliability, outstanding customer service, and outstanding access to outsourcing IT activities, but that this tactic could easily backfire when the product did not meet the unrealistic expectation produced by such hyperbole. Perhaps the outsourcing deal failed because the scope was poorly defined or there was a lack of communication up front with regard to design requirements and the relationship in general. This element was therefore given weight as one of the variables in the proposed study questionnaire.

Investigative Methodology

A number of methodologies may be employed to investigate outcomes of issues concerning client and vendor relationships, culture, and attitudes, but one of the most important of these is the type of questionnaire employed in the present study. Questionnaires and rating scales have been in use for several years. On the other hand, the META Research Group (2003) suggested that IT managers and vendors cooperatively create processes when solving a particular problem. The group further pointed out that as processes proved successful, leading outsourcing vendors could implement new procedures and share best practices, activities which might result in an increase in technology outsourcing success rates.

IT organizations lacking process cultures would find vendor-imposed procedures impractical and burdensome, risking adding outsourcing failure to the existing internal failure risk. By 2004-2005, an increasing percentage of outsourcing contracts were expected to incorporate business services and compliance based on business metrics. Although many IT managers will expect value metrics to increase outsourcing success, they will soon revert to processes for managing long-term vendor results (META Research Group, 2003). These culture processes provide for the ongoing activities that ensure alignment between client needs and the objectives of the vendor's services; they should include regular meetings between account managers and executives of both organizations. Relationship processes also address changes to the baseline scope of work — adding or reducing service levels delivered, typically a tedious and time-consuming activity for both the vendor and the IT organization (Meta Research Group, 2001).

Technical processes focus on the design and on compliance with specifications provided by the IT organization, including the creation of architectural standards, measuring compliance with standards, and jointly designing solutions to problems not anticipated in the base agreement. Moreover, processes specify the steps required for agreement on changes between the vendor and the IT organization. Change management is difficult for most companies, and its complexity is compounded when dealing with external vendors. The processes include various forms of service-level reports, depending on the technology sector, the criticality of services, and recent performance (2001).

Summary

This chapter reviewed the literature pertinent to issues of vendor and client relationships, culture, and attitudes. Descriptive research has demonstrated that issues associated with client-vendor relationships and organizational structures have become an important element in management strategy for meeting company objectives. Outsourcing problems are complex and entail considerable implications for the strategy of the firm. Clients and vendors approach outsourcing with different philosophies.

The majority of problems with outsourcing deals are caused by poor communication and lack of effort in the process. According to Rollinson, Broadfield, and Edwards (1998), when outsourcing relationships failed, it was most often caused by a misunderstanding between the client's expectations and the perceived results. The review of the literature emphasized the central importance of communication (Rollinson, Broadfield, & Edwards, 1998). Mullin (1996) noted that the lack of communication is currently based on issues predetermined by the client and vendor. Chapter 3 describes the methodology employed to suggest a problem solution and the major variables of the investigation.

CHAPTER 3:
METHODOLOGY

The first two chapters introduced the problem of the study and reviewed the pertinent literature. The purpose of this descriptive study was to investigate the impact on productivity and client satisfaction levels of the client's and vendor's respective understanding of each other's organizational values and culture (specifically within the IT department) and to investigate which issues and concerns most significantly determine the consequent decisions made by the two parties. This chapter will present and discuss the methodology employed to address the study objectives. The following subsections deal specifically with the research method, sample, data collection methods, instrumentation, and data analysis methodology.

Research Design and Approach

The purpose of a descriptive research project is sample a particular population to ascertain its attitudes or behaviors related to an issue and generalize from that sample inferences that can be made about some characteristic, attitude, or behavior of the larger population. Babbie (1999) says that descriptive research is aimed at describing the characteristics of subjects (vendor and client for the purpose of this study) usually in one of two forms: (a) survey research, or (b) observational research. Descriptive research involves gathering data that describe features such as client and vendor relationship, culture, and attitudinal issues. In the present case, data were organized, tabulated, and analyzed. The independent variable was the employees' respective (client or vendor) organizations. The dependent variables were the employees' perceptions of each other's organizational values and culture and the impact of these perceptions on productivity and client satisfaction. A structured questionnaire was used to gather data from the employees regarding client and vendor relationships, culture, and attitudinal issues as they were perceived to influence organizational outsourcing success or failure.

Survey Research

Survey research may be the most frequently used mode of observation in the social sciences (Babbie, 1999). This popularity most likely is due to the survey's versatility, for it is a method appropriate for all three of the most common research purposes—exploration and description. Babbie (1999) indicated that while although it is useful to distinguish between these three common research purposes, they are rarely mutually exclusive. In other words, studies usually seek to explore, describe, and explain to varying degrees ,as does the present study. The survey that achieves all three is probably the best method available for describing a population that is too large to observe directly (p. 234).

A well-designed survey can provide a snapshot of the attitudes, beliefs, or behaviors of a group of people at a particular point in time. Exploratory and descriptive studies are usually based on the cross-sectional design (Babbie, 1999). Described simply, this design consists of a population, a random selection from the population, and a first and only measurement of the dependent variable. In survey research of this design, there is no independent variable (Grinnell, 1993). This present study followed the randomized cross-sectional survey design, taking a snapshot of the vendor and client by surveying their attitudes, beliefs, and behaviors regarding IT. The dependent variables in the study were organizational structure (the extent to which the client and vendor employees understood the objective) and the culture.

Questionnaires and rating-scales of the type used in this study have been in use for over a century (Babbie, 1999). The advantages of questionnaires include anonymity, low administrative cost, easy comparison and analysis of data, and simplicity of administration to many people; therefore, a significant quantity of data that can be collected. A structured questionnaire, moreover, is more versatile, economical, and efficient when compared with observations or interviews (Leedy, 1997; Rea & Parker, 1997). The disadvantages, beyond its impersonal nature, are that the wording of items can produce biased or uncomprehending responses, that responses may not be made carefully, and that the whole picture may be lost in the detail (1997). Because of these, the research approach consisted of the following steps:

1. Literature review. Here, the aim was to extract from the relevant literature some fundamental issues which could then form the basis of the specific questions making up the survey instrument.

2. Validate the instructions and identify any problems with the draft questionnaire by using a pilot test, administered to a sample group of 5 client-employees and 5 vendor employees. The survey was revised as necessary, based on the pilot test results. The reliability of the data was demonstrated through stable and consistent replication of findings on repeated measurement. Consistency of measurement is determined according to whether the set of items used to measure a phenomenon is highly related (associated with each other) and

measure the same concept (Schneider& Wilson, 1978). Since each of the items is designed to measure the same concept (with slightly different aspects of the concept being dealt with by specific items), it is assumed that a reliable set of items will have a relatively high average inter-item correlation.

3. The validated survey was administered to those from the target populations of client and vendor employees who agreed to participate.

4. The raw response data were tallied and then analyzed using the statistical package (SPSS). SPSS procedure allowed the researcher to examine the relationship between the client and vendor. Frequencies and descriptive are useful procedures for summarizing information about one variable, but the crosstabs procedure generated more information about the relationship between the two variables. Using crosstabs, both variables were measured on a nominal or ordinal scale. The crosstabs procedure created a table that contained a cell for each possible combination of the categories included in the two variables. Inside each cell was the number of cases that fit that particular combination of responses. The researcher instructed SPSS to report on the row, column, and total percentages for each cell of the table.

5. The researcher drew conclusions, identified implications, and made recommendations based on the findings.

Sample and Data Collection

The potential population consisted of the client and vendor employees. There were 2,000 client employees (administrative professionals, scientists, managers and researchers) and 1,000 vendor employees (engineers, managers, computer specialists, IT specialists, and technicians). A stratified sampling procedure was used. A total of 125 clients (n_1) from the employee workgroup and 125 (n_2) from the vendor employee workgroup agreed to participate. The stratified sample consisted of 250 participants ($N = 250$). The surveys were distributed at weekly staff meetings of the respective groups of employees, with the survey given to every 3rd person who entered the room. According to Cornett and Buckner (1975), a sample size of 152 is appropriate with a population of 250.

A sample of fewer than 40 participants is not amenable to certain statistical computations, and 250 would be the standard number for a 5% error (Cornett & Beckner, 1975). In most studies, a 5% sampling error is acceptable (Babbie, 1998; Zikmund, 2000). All surveys conducted to measure one or more variables will be subject to some form of error. Sampling error arises out of the variability that occurs by chance because a random sample, rather than an entire population, is surveyed. A total of 125 employees from each agreed to participate by returning their surveys. This represented a response rate between 50% and 60%.

A 25% response rate from each group would have been above average for survey returns, and if only 40 respondents had been obtained for each group, that would still have constituted a representative sample (Babbie, 1998; Rea & Parker, 1997). It is therefore believed that the number of respondents represented a meaningful sample. Following are the sample sizes needed from a given population (see Table 1).

Table 1:
Sample Sizes for Given Populations

N^a	s^b	N	n
1000	278	250	152
1500	306	260	155
2000	322	270	159
2600	335	280	162
3000	341	290	165
3500	346		
4000	351		

N = population size

$^s n$ = minimum sample size at alpha = .05

The following procedure was adopted with the approval of the Walden University Institutional Review Board.

1. Prior to regular weekly staff meeting, 2000 client and 1,000 vendor employees were notified by e-mail that 15 to 20 minutes had been set aside for the survey. Employees were also informed that the records of the study would be kept private in a locked file to which only the researcher would have access.

2. Upon entering the conference room, employees were handed a survey package, which included the survey and a cover letter that explained the purpose of the study, gave instructions for completing it, and set out ways for returning the completed survey. The client and vendor employees completed the survey.

3. Surveys were handed out weekly until the researcher received a representative sample of 250 surveys. One hundred twenty-five client employees and 125 vendor employees completed the survey and dropped the survey package into a box before leaving the room.

Instrumentation

The Outsourcing IT Questionnaire (see Appendix B) was used to measure responses from 125 client employees and 125 vendor employees regarding relationships, cultures, and attitudinal issues. The survey was divided into three sections. Section 1 consisted of 15 questions or statements and Section 2 comprised 5 statements, each requiring a response in the form of a 5-point Likert-type scale. Section 3 consisted of open questions.

Section 1 was designed to determine how the client and vendor employees respectively viewed the relationship and cultural issues within the organization. Section 2 was designed to determine the perceptions of the client and vendor of the success of the projects and client satisfaction. Section 3 was designed to elicit employees' perceptions of themselves in their own organizations. Careful attention was paid to the wording of the items to reduce distortion arising out of cultural or language differences among respondents. Each section contained a section for comments to gather additional material on the relationships, cultural issues, and concerns of the client and vendor.

The 5-point Likert-type scale provided an efficient and effective means of quantifying the data and obtaining shades of perception. Choices (or categories of response) were in the range of 1 to 5: *strongly disagree* to *strongly agree*. This allowed a form of measurement of the employees' perceptions of relationships, cultures, and attitudes.

As already noted, the items making up the first and second sections were based on information from the literature review. For example, Dewett and Jones (2001) concluded that success and failure are commonly tied to the discipline of organizational effectiveness and, as the IT industry matures, it becomes increasingly relevant to look at relationships of client and vendor groups in terms of organizational principles; several of the survey items were devoted to such relationships. Schmidt (1990) noted that beyond individual performance, the success of a business organization depends upon communication, trust, and leadership; several items related to this observation, as well. Contractor abandonment and on-time delivery were two other factors of importance identified by U. G. Gupta and A. Gupta (1992a, 1992b); items relating to these factors were included. Since nearly half of all outsourcing projects are not delivered on time, and contractors abandon a third of them, a number of items were related to this area to determine if the perceptions of client and vendor respondents are similar.

The survey was developed under the supervision and guidance of the dissertation chair, a faculty member familiar with this area of study. Based on his responses, the researcher modified the questionnaire, and it was this modified survey that was used in the pilot study. The 5 client and 5 vendor employees who agreed to complete the pilot survey were also asked to comment on the item contents as well as on the survey's overall readability, clarity, and ease of completion, and to suggest revisions or additions. The survey items and instructions were revised in response to their commentary.

Instructions that the survey must be completely filled out and that the survey would remain anonymous were also included. Participants' rights were protected in two ways. First, permission was obtained from the client contracting officer and the vendor contracting officer to administer the survey. Second, to ensure anonymity, responses were given to a contracting officer, who forwarded each of the sealed envelope responses to the researcher.

The goal of writing a survey item is to word it in such a way that every potential respondent will interpret it identically, which is, of course, an unachievable ideal. Survey item developers must also keep in mind how much information people are able to recall and to avoid specificity that exceeds the respondent's potential for offering an accurate, ready-made answer (Babbie, 1998). In this case, content validity was established in the following manner: (a) items would be constructed based on the literature review; (b) advisors and colleagues were asked to read and comment on content and readability; and (c) the pilot study was conducted. According to Babbie, reliability involves whether a particular technique applied repeatedly would yield the same (consistent) results each time it is applied to the same object, as long as what is being measured is not changing. For the purpose of this study, the researcher reviewed internal consistency used to measure coefficient or Chronbach's alpha.

Methodology and Data Analysis

The questions to be investigated were as follows:

1. Are there differences between client and vendor employees in their respective perceptions of each other's organizational values and culture within the IT department of an organization?

> H_0 1: There are no differences between client and vendor employees in their respective perceptions of each others' organizational values and culture within the IT department of an organization as measured by the items in Section 1 of the Outsourcing IT Survey.

2. Do any such differences impact client and vendor employees' respective perceptions concerning successful completion of outsourcing tasks?

H_o 2: The differences impact client and vendor employees' perceptions concerning successful completion of outsourcing tasks.

3. Do such differences impact client and vendor employees' respective perceptions concerning client satisfaction?

H_o3: The differences impact client and vendor employees' perceptions concerning client satisfaction.

The client and vendor responses were compared on items in Section 1 (relationship issues) and Section 2 (success issues). Table 2 provides a listing of variables that were assessed in Sections 1 and 2 of the survey.

Table 2:
Variables

Issue	Items/Numbers
1. Relationship	
2. Communication process in place	1
3. Vendor/client understanding	2, 3
4. Vendor/client understanding of vendor/ client responsibilities/services	4, 5, 6, 7
5. Vendor understood client organization— internal processes	8
6. Client understood vendor practices — political environment	9, 10
7. Value of outsourcing to client	11
8. Process in place to communicate client/ vendor concerns	12, 13
9. Processes in place to measure client/ vendor service	14, 15
10. Tasks performed successfully	1
11. Client productivity increased	2
12. Client expectations met	3
13. Lack of understanding client/vendor	4, 5

Because the item responses formed a nominal scale, the number and percentage for each response were calculated for each item. Chi-square analyses performed on each item contained in Sections 2 and 3 were tested for differences between client and vendor responses. Table 3 displays a template for the tables used in the chi-square analysis. The dependent variables were the responses to items and the independent variables were the type of employee (client or vendor).

Table 3:
Chi-square Tables Template

Response	C	n	%	Client node	Vendor %
Strongly Disagree	1	XX	XX.X	XX	XX.X
Disagree	2	XX	XX.X	XX	XX.X
Neutral	3	XX	XX.X	XX	XX.X
Agree	4	XX	XX.X	XX	XX.X
Strongly Agree	5	XX	XX.X	XX	XX.X

According to statistical sources, chi-square analysis reveals differences, if any, between the two groups on survey item responses (Babbie, 1998; Rea & Parker, 1997). It is the most popular and widely used nonparametric test of significance and is particularly useful in tests involving nominal data such as those provided by this survey. When chi-square is used, there is a different distribution for each number of degrees of freedom, defined as the number of categories in the rows minus one times the number of categories in the columns minus 1 ($df = (r - 1)(c - 1)$). The numbers in each cell, depending upon the number of degrees of freedom, must be of sufficient size to ensure that the chi-square test is appropriate. Each expected frequency should be at least five in size when the degree of freedom is equal to one.

In addition, a content analysis was performed on the open-ended response in section 3 of the survey, using a Likert-type scale. Content analysis is a coding operation that may be applied to virtually any form of communication (Patton, 1987). The content analysis for this study consisted of the following specific steps:

1. Read through responses to obtain a list of factors respondents indicated were important and not already elicited by the survey items.

2. Assign a code to each factor.

3. Count the number of times each code was noted.

For the sake of confidentiality and protection of participants, the records of this research study have been kept and will remain private. In any report of this study that might be published, the researcher will not include any information that will make it possible to identify a participant. Research records will be kept in a locked file only the researcher can open.

Summary

Chapter 3 described the methodology employed to assemble and analyze the data collected by means of a survey questionnaire. This chapter also described the test instrument used by the researcher and administered at scheduled weekly meetings. Chapter 4 presents the collected information and analyzes the data derived from administration of the questionnaire survey instrument.

CHAPTER 4:
RESULTS

This study was designed to investigate whether differences in institutional culture and attitude affected client and vendor relationships and to determine if perceptions of such factors affected productivity and client satisfaction over the outsourcing of IT in an organization. This chapter presents the results in an introduction followed by analysis of the survey responses. Dewett and Jones (2001) concluded that success and failure were commonly tied to the discipline of organizational effectiveness and that, as the IT industry matured, it would become increasingly relevant to look at relationships of client and vendor groups in terms of organizational principles. On-time delivery and contractor abandonment and were two other factors of importance identified by Cunningham (1999) and U. G. Gupta, and A. Gupta, (1992a, 1992b); they were therefore taken into account in the survey.

Presentation of Data

The traditional Pearson correlation chi-square statistic testing was employed to analyze the data collection because it could show the strength of the relationship between the variables and indicate the existence of the relationship. Chi-square was used to look at the statistical significance of an association between a categorical outcome and a categorical determining variable. Correlation was also employed to analyze data because it provided an analysis that could stand on its own, because it underlies many other analyses, and it served to be an accurate way to support conclusions after primary analyses were completed. Correlations are a measure of the linear relationship between two variables. Table 4 displays the extent of agreement between the two groups over matters of organizational values and cultures. Table 5 displays the extent of agreement between the two groups as to the overall success of outsourcing. Table 6 displays the relative weighting given by the two groups to different kinds of factor for the non-renewal of contracts.

Table 4:

Extent of Vendor and Client Agreement Regarding Organizational Values and Cultures

	Vendors $n=125$		Clients $n=125$		
	n	%	n	%	p
1. A process was in place to communicate quality issues with the vendor.	87	69.6	86	68.8	.89
2. The vendor clearly understood expectations.	92	73.4	93	74.4	.63
3. The client clearly understood expectations.	114	91.2	115	92.0	.82
4. The vendor understood client responsibilities.	115	92.0	81	64.8	.001
5. The client understood vendor responsibilities.	117	93.6	119	95.2	.58
6. The vendor understood client services.	111	88.8	71	56.8	.001
7. The client understood vendor services.	120	96.0	121	96.8	.73

8. The vendor understood the client's internal processes.	70	56.0	62	49.6	.31
9. The client lacked understanding of the vendor's political environment.[a]	108	86.4	113	90.4	.32
10. The client lacked understanding of vendor practices. [a]	15	12.0	37	29.6	.001
11. Outsourcing was valuable to the client.	66	52.8	125	100.0	.001
12. Not aware of process to communicate vendor's quality concerns.[a]	64	24.0	84	51.2	.001
13. Not aware of process to communicate client's quality concerns.[a]	77	15.0	120	61.6	.001
14. Process in place to measure client's levels of service.	95	76.0	125	100.0	.001
15. Process in place to measure vendor's levels of service.	81	64.8	125	100.0	.001

Note. Statements are paraphrased from original survey.

[a] Frequency and percentage of respondents who "Disagree" or Strongly Disagree"

Questionnaire data analyzed with SPSS.

$N = 250$

Table 5:

Extent of Vendor and Client Agreement Regarding
Successful Completion of Outsourcing Tasks

	Vendors n=125		Clients n=125		
	n	%	n	125	p
1. Majority of time the client's requirements are reasonable.	114	91.2	124	99.2	.003
2. Client's productivity increased by outsourcing.	117	93.6	124	99.2	.02
4. Most of time results meet client's expectations.	121	96.8	84	67.2	.001
5. Most of time vendor is successful at performing tasks.	118	94.4	63	50.4	.001
Note. Statements are paraphrased from original survey. Survey data analyzed with SPSS					

N= 250

Table 6:

Reasons Given by Vendors and Clients
Concerning Client Satisfaction

	Vendors n=125		Clients n=125		
	n	%	n	%	p
1. Reasons client would not renegotiate					
pertaining to culture	56	86.2	47	73.4	.072
pertaining to personalities	34	52.3	32	50.0	.793
pertaining to communication	51	78.5	53	82.8	.532

2. Reasons vendor would not renegotiate					
pertaining to culture	65	84.8	22	34.4	.001
pertaining to personalities	43	66.2	46	71.9	.482
pertaining to communication	59	90.8	19	29.7	.001
3. Circumstances not mentioned that client and vendor would not renegotiate contract					
pertaining to culture	61	44.8	84	17.6	.001
pertaining to personalities	31	47.7	32	50.0	.931
pertaining to communication	34	47.2	64	70.3	.000

$N= 250$

The responses in Tables 4, 5, and 6 clearly demonstrate significant differences. Monitoring processes should provide for ongoing activities that assess, adjust, and optimize alignment between client needs and the objectives of the vendor's services; they should include regular meetings between account managers and executives of both organizations (Davidson, 2001). It has been observed, however, that in practice clients and vendors rarely discuss their philosophies and the impact that they will have on the relationship.

Analysis of Survey Questions

The following sections provide an analysis of the data collected by means of the survey instrument. The survey responses permitted a general overview of the degree to which culture and attitude affected client and vendor relationships. Further, the survey examined whether respondents agreed or disagreed regarding the presence of significant differences between client and vendor groups in their respective perceptions of each other's attitudes and cultural values, such as might affect successful outsourcing of IT by reducing vendor productivity and client satisfaction.

Table 4 displays the extent of agreement or disagreement between the two groups (vendor employees and client employees) regarding perceptions of each other's requirements and responsibilities, communications, organizational values, and cultures. The extent of agreement was defined as the percentage of respondents who answered *agree* or *strongly agree* to a survey item.

Item 4 asked whether vendor employees understood the client's requirements and 92.0% of the vendors, as compared to 64.8% of the clients, agreed or strongly agreed. This difference was significant (p = .001).

Item 6 asked whether vendor employees understood the client's services, and 88.8% of the vendors, as compared to 56.8% of the clients, either agreed or strongly agreed. This difference was significant (p = .001).

Item 10 asked whether there were significant differences in the client understanding of vendor practices: the opinions of 12% of the vendors, compared to 29.6 % of the clients, were in either disagreement or strong disagreement. This difference was significant (p = .001).

Item 11 queried whether, in respondents' opinions, outsourcing had been valuable to the client: Only 53% of the client employees, compared with 100% of the vendor employees, agreed or strongly agreed. This difference was significant (p = .001).

Item 12 assessed awareness, on the respondents' part, of any process for communicating the client's quality concerns to the vendor: 34% of the vendor employees, as compared to 53% of the client employees, were not aware on any such process (i.e., disagreed or strongly disagreed with the item's positive affirmation). This difference was significant ($p = .001$).

Item 13 tested for awareness of a process by which the client would communicate quality concerns to the vendor. Although 62% of the client employees said they were concerned about the quality, as few as 15% of their vendor counterparts agreed. This difference was significant ($p = .001$).

Item 14 asked whether a process was in place to measure the client's level of service: 76% of the vendor employees, as compared to 100.0% of the client employees, either agreed or strongly agreed. This difference was significant. ($p = .001$).

Item 15 asked whether a process was in place to measure the vendor's level of service: 65% of the vendor employees, as compared to 100.0% of the client employees, either agreed or strongly agreed with that statement. This difference was significant ($p = .001$).

No other chi-square comparison in Table 4 between the two groups was significant at the $p = .05$ level.

Table 5 displays the degrees of agreement and disagreement between vendor and client employees regarding successful completion of outsourcing tasks. The survey items related to their respective perceptions of the service provided by the vendor to the client.

Item 1 was to assess whether, in their respective employees' opinions, majority of the time the client's requirements are reasonable: 91% of the vendor employees, compared to 99.2% of the client employees, either agreed or strongly agreed. There was no significant difference ($p = .003$).

Item 2 was to assess opinions as to whether the client's productivity was increased by outsourcing: 94% of the vendor employees, as compared to 99.2% of the client employees, either agreed or strongly agreed. There was no significant difference ($p = .02$).

Item 4 was to assess opinions as to whether most of the time the results of outsourcing met the client's expectations, and 96.8% of the vendor employees, compared with 67.2% of the client employees, either agreed or strongly agreed. This was a significant difference (p = .001).

Item 5 identified a significant disagreement. Asked whether most of the time the vendor was successful in performing its tasks, 94% of the vendors, compared to only 50.4% of the clients, agreed or strongly agreed. This was a significant difference (p = .001).

Table 6 displays a content-standardized version of the additional types of factor identified by vendor employees and client employees to account for client satisfaction or dissatisfaction. Item 3 asked, "Under what circumstances that has not been mentioned in this survey would you be more inclined to renegotiate a contract? Three different, broad themes, clarified by content analysis, were represented in the responses: there were reasons pertaining to cultural differences, to personal differences, and to problems in communication. There were significant gaps between the two groups in their perceptions of the reasons why clients and vendors might not renegotiate their contract.

The respondents were asked to identify any other factors they felt would cause vendors not to renegotiate a contract and, again, the responses were classified under the three broad headings: those pertaining to culture, to personalities, and to communication difficulties. Culture was indicated by 44.8% of the vendors to be s, compared to 17.6% of the clients. This difference was significant (p = .001). Communication problems were indicated by 47.2% of the vendors, compared to 70.3% of the clients. Again, the difference was significant (p = .001).

Survey items 1 through 15, in section 1, were focused on perceptions of institutional culture and attitude, and items 1 through 5, in section 2, on perceptions of productivity and client satisfaction. Section 3, Items 1 through 3, offered the invitation to the vendor and the client employees to expand, in unstructured, open-ended form, on their perceptions of the reasons contracts were not renewed. Three primary categories of cause were adopted for analyzing the responses: those pertaining to institutional culture, personalities, and communication between the parties. As revealed by their responses (Table 6), there were significant differences of perception and opinion between the two groups.

Using research questions 1, 2, and 3 as the framework for the study, the Pearson chi-square technique was employed to analyze the data collection. A .05 confidence level was used in the data analysis for each survey question. Tables 4, 5, and 6 show the statistical test results for research questions 1, 2, and 3. The following sections pertain to the findings of the study.

Findings

The findings returned by the survey instrument indicated some statistically significant differences between client and vendor perceptions of the success and failure of outsourcing contracts, as assessed within the three categories: culture, personalities, and communication. Section 3, question 3: Significant differences existed with respect to client satisfaction. This result appears to support the view that in a good relationship the client's expectations and objectives should be clearly defined and reasonable. The objectives and expectations of a good relationship require a suitable cultural mix whereby both parties communicate effectively with each other.

Summary

Chapter 4 included tabular presentations of the data resulting from the analyses of the responses from the survey instrument. Chapter 5 presents a summary of the findings and recommendations for further research in the field of improving the efficacy of outsourcing IT and the client-vendor outsourcing relationship that bears heavily on whether it is beneficial to both entities.

CHAPTER 5:
SUMMARY, CONCLUSIONS, AND RECOMMENDATIONS

The researcher conducted this study to determine if there are differences between the client and vendor employees involved in an IT outsourcing arrangement in their respective perceptions of the organizational values and culture within the IT department of each other's organization. The study examined whether or not cultural and attitudinal differences impacted such perceptions, particularly as they related to the successful completion of outsourcing tasks. It also explored whether or not cultural differences might impact client and vendor employees' respective perceptions of client satisfaction. There is evidence to support the contention that the client and vendor must do more in order to ensure the perception of the employee do not adversely affect the success of the IT outsourcing agreement.

This result appears to support the view that managing the overall relationship is the area where the greatest effort is required. It is here that problems are most likely to occur and where the relationship management should go beyond addressing the provision of products and services and move into the realm of compatibility, which is often overlooked as nonessential (not relating to products, services, or pricing) yet is often the source of client dissatisfaction. Based on the findings of this study, evidence supports the view that the nature of the relationship and the effectiveness of the intercommunication between client and vendor could substantially determine the success or abandonment of an IT outsourcing agreement.

The data analysis revealed that some significant differences existed between client and vendor responses to certain items covered by the survey instrument (see Tables 4 and 5). Additionally, data analysis revealed that significant differences existed with respect to culture and communications, with significant implications for the willingness of the client to renegotiate (Section 3, items 1 and 2). Moreover, divergent perceptions were found between the client and vendor employees respectively regarding each other's organizational values and culture within the IT department. There were significant differences in the client and vendor perceptions of how well the client understood the vendor's practices (Section 1, Item 12). Accordingly, it is necessary to develop an awareness of the ways in which culture differs and how these differences affect interactions between the clients and vendors.

There were significant differences between the client's and the vendor's perceptions of whether the vendor was performing a task successfully (Section 1, Item 15). Having an established metrics would provide the client and vendor with a benchmark to measure against (Pinnington & Woolcock, 1997). It would be desirable for a client organization to establish precise, measurable objectives, document expected improvements, create a scorecard, and implement a regular review process (Dun & Bradstreet, 2000). Further, in order to minimize conflicts and problems within a partnership between client and vendor, it would be important for the two to establish a common goal at the outset (1997).

Open responses and written comments led to the conclusion that there were significant differences between the parties as to the effectiveness of any existing process to communicate one's quality concerns to the other and vice versa (Sections 1, 2, and 3). Managing the overall relationship would seem to be the area where the greatest effort is required because it is here that problems are most likely to occur. The reason is that relationship management addresses areas beyond the provision of products and services and deal with elements of compatibility, which are often overlooked as nonessential but which have emerged, in this study, as an area of critical importance.

The following interpretation of findings are drawn from proportion of survey responses that emphasized differences between client and vendor perceptions of each other's organizational values and culture, a mismatch that was apparently having a negative effect on the vendor's productivity and the client's satisfaction levels. Every organization seeks more efficient and more cost effective strategies, but some companies ignore the potential problems that may accompany outsourcing. The allure of outsourcing as a way to address company inefficiencies or budgetary concerns may blind management to the potential dangers of shifting an internal process to outside contractors.

The data were investigated using consistency of measurement that determined whether the set of survey items used to measure a phenomenon were highly related (associated with each other) and measured the same concept. The data were also investigated using client and vendor categories. There were significant differences of perception between the client and the vendor respondents (see Table 4), with notably significant differences shown for Items 6, 10, 11, 12, 13, and 15. No other chi-square comparison in Table 4 between the two groups was significant at the $p = .05$ level. This seems to indicate that many organizations may not be managing outsourcing transition in a way that delivers a satisfactory outcome.

Interpretation of Findings

The survey was also designed to ascertain whether differences between client and vendor employees' perceptions of each other's organizational values and culture had a negative effect on vendor productivity and client satisfaction. The client and vendor need to be aware of the other party's expectations. There were significant differences of perception between the two groups (see Table 5) as to the other's expectations and level of satisfaction. Various levels of agreements (Q1, 2, and 3) and the level of significant differences, as revealed by chi-square analysis, disagreements were notably high (Q4 and 5).

One implication seemed to be that relationships could fail because vendors did not fully understand what their requirements were. There is evidence to support the contention that one of the first risks to consider is the possible tension between client and vendor employees arising out of different institutional relationships, attitudes, and cultures. Managing and meeting client expectations in outsourcing is a major challenge in IT-enabled outsourcing services., Earl (1996), and Hoffman and Klepper (2000) observed that organizational culture is relevant to outsourcing success. Although the distinction may seem insignificant, the connotation of a relationship is that the parties are dependent on each other for the success of their mutual projects; this is important and should be valued by the client and vendor. It takes two parties to have a partnership.

Survey responses were solicited relating to the self-perception of the vendor. Content analysis was used with the open-ended questions to identify any further observations reported by the client and vendor subjects about each other's organizational values and culture. Significant differences were evident in their perceptions of each other's culture and communication as factors in the failure to renew contracts (see Table 6, Items 1 and 2). The highest level of difference was found with respect to communication: Q1, client (30%) and vendor (91%); compare Question 2 (Culture): client (22%) and vendor (56%). Notable conclusion of the interpretation of findings indicated that in order for companies to ensure success of IT outsourcing the companies must cultivate an organization built on enduring relationships and communication within the client and vendor employees.

According to Sheth and Sobel (2004), the organizations should develop shared personal knowledge about each other that enables client and vendor to talk about things other than business and to enjoy interactions on a personal level. Building personal relationships will enhance the client relationship. Second, the vendor will develop a better understanding of clients' goals. Americans, for example, are comfortable doing business with someone they do not know very well but who meet certain professional criteria and standards. In southern Europe, Latin America, and parts of Asia, it can work differently: People often will not do business with anyone they do not know personally.

Implications for Social Change

Positive social change is the expression of a group's action to alter behavior or practices that affect the organization and the process of forming new beliefs and perceptions (Wollman, Lobenstine, Foderaro, & Stose, 1998). Research indicates that one way to change the organization is to change the climate of the organization. Since both technological and culture change are inevitable, organizations will have to learn to adapt to other cultures. Some examples of positive organizational social changes are accomplished by increasing competitiveness, increasing market share, reducing customer complaints, listening to the customer, and cultivating the relationship (Wollman et al., 1998).

McGregor (1999) found that for true success, companies must cultivate an organization built on enduring relationships with the workforce and clients, but Maslow (1997) showed that organizational behavior was the product of the actions and attitudes of people in the organization and their perceptions and feelings. It follows that there may be improvement in the client-vendor relationship if these issues are addressed, resulting in a sustainable improvement in performance. Both parties to the relationship must have an appreciation of its value and a commitment to the efforts required to maintain it (Morgan & Hunt, 1994; Moorman, Zaltman, & Deshipand, 1992). Major downsizing and other initiatives that emphasize doing more with less have also had a great impact on organizational change. As companies continue to move to a more decentralized work environment, this already strong trend can only accelerate further and influence social change. Social change process analysis is essential in today's business world for managers to keep up with rapid changes brought on by competition, globalization, and the outsourcing of IT.

Significantly different levels of perception were observed between the client and vendor perceptions of each other's organizational values and culture. The highest level of significant difference occurred in the responses pertaining to communication and culture. There may be improvement in the client and vendor relationship if communication and cultural issues are addressed, resulting in a sustainable improvement in performance. Both parties to the client-vendor relationship must have an appreciation of its value and a commitment to the efforts required to maintain it (Morgan & Hunt, 1994; Moorman et al., 1992).

These results suggest that a successful relationship between client and vendor requires an ongoing assessment that entails the setting and validating of mutual goals and that parties work closely together throughout the term of the relationship. As companies continue to move to a more decentralized work environment, this trend can accelerate further and influence social change. According to the Everest Research Group (2005) Outsourcing is a management option rather than the process of just increasing a company's profit. Companies are outsourcing to reduce or stabilize costs, access advanced technology, compensate the lack of skilled IT workers, improve business efficiency, meet earning projections, tie technology to business value, and remain competitive in the global marketplace. The downturn in the economy has amplified the importance of cost management, leading companies to make cost savings their number one objective in an outsourcing agreement. In addition to this, other significant factors accelerating the growth of the outsourcing market are

1. *Technological competence.* By outsourcing, companies are able to take advantage of new technology that they previously might not have had access to. This includes customized software as well as networking technologies.

2. *Core competencies.* As noncore functions within the company are used for outsourcing to third parties, companies are able to focus on the core competencies central to their value proposition and increase their competitive advantage.

Recommendations for Action

The following recommendations are based primarily on the results of this study, but to some extent they are also influenced by insights gained through the literature review. The researcher engaged in continual effort during the course of this research to keep abreast of continuously changing events in outsourcing IT.

The recommendations and final topic discussions are intended as a contribution to the knowledge base in the aforementioned areas and, it is hoped, as an aid in future decision making regarding outsourcing IT. They may also help to better inform the perceptions held by client and vendor employees of each other's organizational values and culture within their IT departments. Based on the findings, the researcher recommends the following courses of action.

1. Create among key individuals communication protocols. The individual protocol would provide a framework for the secure and confidential sharing of information goals and objectives between the client and vendor. The protocol would create and provide detailed progress reports, documentation, act as the primary interface for all issues pertaining to the project, evaluate staffing needs, and possess communication skills too effectively collaborate with clients and vendors.

Finally, the protocol would identify issues and develop solutions. Where information sharing has occurred, its value has often been reduced by misunderstandings in the use of language or inefficiencies in communication channel.

2. Establish an outsource team before outsourcing service provider is selected. Team members should include a relationship manager, senior executive, financial analyst, and a member from the IT department. Detailed documentation procedures and objectives

should be established at this time. In order to have a well functioning business unit within a company, communication is critical. An outsource team consultant will provide tools and methods to promote staff integration and reduce cultural conflicts. This team should stay in place throughout the contract phase.

3. Develop management training for the client and vendor. Employees should receive cultural training, and key client and vendor managers should visit the offsite facilities in order to improve communication channels that would enhance success. Closing the gap in companies' internal capabilities and investing properly in relationship management skills and processes may lead to the vendor meeting the required level of expectation.

4. Create a positive, open-door climate for the client and vendor for the purpose of presenting work-related concerns and providing effective communications within the organization. This activity could be delegated to senior individuals within the organization. This policy could also provide the senior manager with a significant amount of information that that would otherwise not be known or received in a timely manner. Outsourcing IT processes requires a partnership arrangement between client and vendor. The foundation is thereby laid for greater productivity.

5. Study the cultural capability of the vendor prior to selection. This process would include conducting a due diligence process, performing capability assessments, performing a readiness assessment, working with project managers, monitoring service level agreements, and measuring past client satisfaction. The vendor's expertise and technologies should not be the only motivator when selecting a provider. Selecting the right partner is critical to the success of the partnership.

6. Monitor the client satisfaction process by updating performance measurements. This process involves establishing performance plans, baseline, and benchmarks as well as analysis. Regularly scheduled service level reviews should be conducted to ensure appropriate level of management oversight.

7. Hire a project manager to assess the technical capabilities of the vendor for any project that is larger than one developer. This person would lead the development project by taking ownership of the program and would be entrusted with the project budget and held accountable for the project deliverables. An additional responsibility would be assessing vendors as to their experience in a given field, availability of qualified personnel with diversified skills in hardware and software, and the availability of corporate support groups.

Recommendations for Further Study

One question for future research is how the client and vendor can share their perceptions and balance their goals and objectives. This area of research has been often overlooked or downplayed. Another avenue for developing new theories of outsourcing relationships is the need for detailing and interpreting cultural metrics for measuring cost and the service performance of the vendor. Future research could investigate the cost associated with outsourcing: the lag time to adapt to market changes, the loss of technical expertise, and extended development times due to cultural differences. Such field research could provide validation and framework.

Conclusion

Soon, there will likely be new reasons why companies are looking to outsource, new types of outsourcing relationships, and new reasons certain providers are chosen. Growth in global outsourcing will transform the U.S. workforce. Managers will need to have increased awareness of the client and the vendor employee groups about why and how cross-cultural differences in relationships, culture and attitude, and expectations affect work interactions and effectiveness. This researcher has developed a framework for adoption of policies, practices, and strategies for addressing these issues in order to maximize profits and future growth.

References

Anderson, J. (1983). *The architecture of cognition.* Cambridge, MA: Harvard University Press.

Antonucci, Y. L., Lordi, F. C., & Tucker, J. J., III (1998). The pros and cons of IT outsourcing. *Journal of Accountancy, 185*(6), 26-31.

Antonucci, Y. L., & Tucker, J. J., III. (1998). IT outsourcing: Current trends, benefits, and risks. *Information Strategy: The Executive's Journal, 14*(2), 16-26.

Asbrand, D. (1997a). Outsource your maintenance migraines. *Datamation, 43,* 50-54.

Asbrand, D. (1997b). Outsourcing becomes strategic, *Datamation* 43-73.

Babbie, E. R. (1998). *The practice of social research..* Belmont, CA: Wadsworth/Thomson.

Barrett, R. (1996). Outsourcing success means making the right moves. Retrieved January 2004, from http://www.reegineering.com/articles/July 96/ InforManagement.html

Benko, C. (1992). If information systems outsourcing is the solution, What is the problem? *Journal of Systems Management, 43*(11), 32-35.

Benko, C. (1993). Outsourcing evaluation: A profitable process, *Information Systems Management, 10*(2), 45-50.

Berelson, B. (1974). Content analysis in communication research. New York: Free Press.

Cash, J. I., & Konsynski, B. R. (1994). IS redraws competitive boundaries? *Harvard Business Review, 1,* 134-142.

Cheon, M., Grover, V., & Teng, J. (1995). Theoretical perspectives on the outsourcing of information systems, *Journal of Information Technology, 10*(4), 209-220.

Cole-Gomolski, B. (1998). Bulgarian outsourcer courts U.S. market. *Computerworld,* 32-33.

Cornett, J. D., & Beckner, W. (1975). *Introductory statistics for the behavioral sciences,* Columbus, OH: Charles Merrill.

Cronk, J., & Sharp, J. (1999). A framework for deciding what to outsource in information technology, *Journal of Information Technology, 10*(4), 259-267.

Dataquest Research Study. (2003). Human Resources and Outsourcing. Retrieved January 2004 from http://search.yahoo.com/search?p=Dataquest+2003+outsourcing+report&fr=fp-pull-web-t&*n*=20&fl=0&x=wrt

Davidson, D. (2001). META Research Group report, Retrieved March 20, 2004, from http://computerworld.com.my/pcwmy.nsf/ unidlookup/ OB5A3E9D2C6F1E9748256BA400175FF?

Dewett, T., & Jones, G. (2001). The role of information technology in the organization: A review, model, and assessment. *Journal of Management: Managing in the Information Age, 27*(3), 313-346.

Drucker, P. (1995). *Managing in a time of great change.* New York: Dutton.

Dun & Bradstreet Barometer of Global Outsourcing. (2000).. Retrieved January 2003 from http://www.c-people.com/c-interest/c-interest8.html.

Duncan, N. B. (1995a). *Buying core competencies: A study of the impact of outsourcing on IT infrastructure flexibility.* Retrieved March 2004 from http://hsb.baylor.edu/ ramsower/acis/papers/ duncan.html.

Duncan, N. B. (1995b). Capturing IT infrastructure flexibility: A study of resource characteristics and their measure. *Journal of Management Information Systems, 12*(2), 55-67.

Earl, M. J. (1996). The risks of outsourcing IT. *Sloan Management Review, 37*(3), 26-32.

Edberg, D., Grupe, F., & Kuechler, W. (2001). *Practical issues in global IT management 18,* 51-60.

Everest Partners Group. (2005). *International outsourcing.* Retrieved February 20, 2005, from http://www.outsourcing-offshore.com/contracting.html,

Farmer, D. W. (1990). *Strategies for change: Managing change in higher education.* San Francisco: Jossey-Bass.

Fee, T. (2001). Client management. Retrieved March 2004 from http://www.procentral.com/articles/ClientManagement.html

Feurer, R., Chaharbaghi, K., Weber, M., & Wargin, J. (2000). *Aligning strategies, processes, and IT: A case study.* Boca Raton, FL: Auerback.

Forrester Research. (2004). *Projected IT growth.* Retrieved December 2003 fromhttp://www.forrester.com/find?N=50175

Gartner Research Group. (2003). *Outsourcing.* Retrieved November 2003 from http://www.gridnine.com/en/news/year2003/04-11.html

Graham, M., & Scarborough, H. (1997). Information technology outsourcing by state governments in Australia. *Australian Journal of Public Administration, 56*(3), 30-39.

Gupta, U. G., & Gupta, A. (1992a). Outsourcing the IS function: Is it necessary for your organization? *Information Systems Management, 9*(3), 44-50.

Guptill, B. (2002). *PRM research group.* Retrieved January 2004 from http://66.218.71.225/ search/cache? P=client vendor +cultural&ei=UTF-8&cop=mss&xargs=0&psta

rt=6&b=21&url =g_ROvLVH5qsJ: www.saugatech.com/
STPerspectives/5-22-02%2520%2520%2520PRM%2520 Res
earch%2520Perspectives%2520WO%2520May%252020.pdf

Guterl, F. (1996). How to manage your outsourcer, *Datamation, 42*,
79-83.

Halvey, J. & Melby, B. (1996). *Information technology outsourcing
transactions, process, strategies, and contracts.* New York:
John Wiley & Sons.

Hatch, M. J., & Schultz, M. (2001). Are the strategic stars aligned
for your corporate brand? *Harvard Business Review, 79*(2),
128-134.

Hoffman, N., & Klepper, R. (Summer 2000). Assimilating new
technologies: The role of organizational culture, *Information
Systems Management, 17.*

Hofstede, G. (1980). *Culture's consequences: International differences
in work-related values.* London: McGraw Hill.

Huber, R. L. (Jan-Feb. 1993) How Continental outsourced its crown
jewels, *Harvard Business Review, 71*(1), 121-129.

Jacobides, M. G. (1998). *Rethinking the impact of information
technology on transaction costs and outsourcing practices.*
Retrieved November 2003 from http://blue.temple.edu/
~eastern/jacobide.html.

Jones, W. (1997). Outsourcing basics. *Information Systems
Management, 14*(1), 66-69.

Kakabadse, N., & Kakabadse, A. (2000). Critical review--Outsourcing: A paradigm shift. *Journal of Management Development, 19*(8), 670-728.

Khosrowpour, M. (Ed.). (1995). *Managing information technology investments with outsourcing.* Hershey, PA: Idea Group.

Khosrowpour, M., Subramanian, G. H., Gunderman, J., & Saber, A. (1996). Managing information technology with outsourcing: An assessment of employee perceptions. *Journal of Applied Business Research, 12*(3), 85-96.

King, J., & Cole-Gomolski, B. (1999). IT doing less development, more installation and outsourcing, *Computer World, 33*(4), 2-3.

King, W. & Malhotra, Y. (2002). Developing a framework for analyzing IS sourcing, *Information & Management, 37,* 323-334.

King, W., & Malhotra, Y. (2000). Developing a framework for analyzing IS Sourcing, *Information & Management, 37,* 323-334.

Kini, R. B. (1996). Technical reports: IS outsourcing beyond the 'bandwagon.' *International Journal of Computer Applications in Technology, 9*(1), 48-52.

Klepper, R. (1995). The management of partnering development in I/S outsourcing. *Journal of Information Technology, 19,* 249-258.

KPMG Consulting Study (1999). Failed IT Projects. Retrieved December 2003 from http://www.nwfusion.com/news/2001/ 1107highmark.html.

Kruger, B. (2000). Success of the outsourcing relationship should be the main objective when establishing a service level agreement. Retrieved November 2003 from http://www.oribi. Net/Articles%5CSuccess.htm

Lacity, M. C., & Hirschheim, R. (1993). Implementing information systems outsourcing: Key issues and experiences of an early adopter. *Journal of General Management, 19*(1), 17-31.

Lacity, M. C., & Hirschheim, R. (2000*). Information systems outsourcing: Myths, metaphors, and realities.* Chichester, England: John Wiley & Sons.

Lee, J. N., & Kim, Y. G. (1999). Effect of partnership quality on IS outsourcing success: Conceptual framework and empirical validation, *Journal of Management Information Systems, 15*(4), 29-61.

Leedy, P. D. (1997). *Practical research: Planning and design* (6th ed.). Upper Saddle River, NJ: Prentice-Hall.

Loh, L., & Venkatraman, N. (1992). Determinants of information technology outsourcing: A cross-sectional analysis. *Journal of Management Information Systems, 9*(1), 7-24.

Marshall, J. (2003). Outsourcing, *Financial Executive, 19*(6), 51-56.

Maslow, A. (1997). *Motivation and personality* (2nd Ed.). New York: Harper & Row.

McClelland, D., McLellan, K., Marcolin, B., & Beamish, P (1995). Financial and strategic motivations behind IS outsourcing. *Journal of Information Technology, 10*(4), 299-322.

McGregor, D. (Ed.). (1999). *Managing the human side of enterprise.* New York: John Wiley & Sons.

META Research Group (2003). Outsourcing and service provider. Retrieved March 2004 from http://www.metagroup.com/products/insights/osps_trends.html

Moorman, C., Zaltman, G., & Deshipand, R. (1992). Relationships between providers and users of marketing research: The dynamics of trust within and between organizations. *Journal of Marketing Research, 29,* 324-329.

Morgan, G. (1997). *Images of organizations,* Thousand Oaks, CA: Sage Publications.

Morgan, R. M., & Hunt, S.D. (1994). The commitment trust theory of relationship marketing, *Journal of Marketing, 58,* 20-38.

Mullin, R. (1996). Outsourcing: Managing the outsourced enterprise, *Journal of Business Strategy, 17*(4), 8-36.

Patton, M. Q. (1987). *Using qualitative methods in evaluation,* Newbury Park, CA: Sage.

Pinnington, A., & Woolcock, P. (1997). The role of vendor companies in IS/IT outsourcing, *International Journal of Information Management, 17*(3), 199-210.

Rea, L. M., & Parker, R. A. (1997). *Designing and conducting survey research: A comprehensive guide* (2nd ed.). San Francisco: Jossey-Bass:.

Rollinson, D., Broadfield, A., & Edwards, D. (1998). *Organizational behavior and analysis: An integrated approach.* Essex, England: Addison Wesley Longman Ltd.

Rosencrance, L. (2003). Outsourcing is the fastest-growing federal technology segment. Retrieved November 2003. http://search. yahoo.com/search? p=Rosencrance+2003+outsourcing&fr=f p-pull-web-t&n=20&fl=0&x=wrt

Ruber, P. (1995), Drive a hard bargain with network outsourcers. *Datamation, 41,* 61-64.

Sabherwal, R. (1999). *The role of trust in outsourced development projects community.* San Francisco: Jossey-Bass, Inc., 130-150.

Schein, E. (2001). *Organizational culture and leadership,* In J. Shafritz, & J. S. Ott (eds.), *Classics of organization theory* (373-380). Fort Worth, TX: Harcourt College Publishers.

Schmidt, F. L., & Judiesch, M. K. (1990). Individual differences in output variability as a function of job complexity, *Journal of Applied Psychology, 75,* 28-42.

Schneider, A. L. & Wilson, L. A. (1978), *Introduction to interrupted time series design*. National Institute, H.W. Wilson Company Publisher, 280-287.

Sheth, J. N., & Sobel, A. C. (2004). *Clients for life: How great professionals develop breakthrough relationships*. Baron Publisher, CA.

Snow, C. P. (1959). *The two cultures*. Great Britain: Cambridge University Press.

Soininen, J. (1997). *A framework for analyzing of outsourcing in the information technology field*, M.Sc. Thesis. University of Waterloo, Ontario, Canada.

Sproull, L. S. (1995). Response effects in the electronic survey, *Public Opinion Quarterly, 50 ,402-403*.

Wollman, N., Lobenstine, M., Foderaro, M. & Stose, S. (1998). *Principles for promoting social change*, Washington, D.C: Society for the Psychological Study of Social Issues.

Willcocks, L., Lacity, M., & Fitzgerald, G. (1995). Information technology outsourcing in Europe and the USA: Assessment issues, *International Journal of Information Management, 15*, 333-351.

Yesulatitis, J. A. (1997). Outsourcing for new technology adoption, *Information Systems Management, 14*(2), 80-82.

Zikmund, W. G. (2000). *Effective marketing: Creating and keeping customers in an e-commerce world*. Pittsburg, PA: Whitmore Publishing Company.

Appendix C
Outsourcing It Survey

The purpose of this survey was to collect data on the differences, if any, between the respective perceptions of client and vendor employees regarding each other's organizational values and culture within the outsourcing Information Technology department of an organization.

The survey is divided into two sections. The first section rates your perception of the client and vendor relationships and culture within the organization. The second section rates your perception of the client service.

Directions: Please answer the questions by placing an X next to the response that provides the answer you consider most accurate. This information is confidential and will be used only in conjunction with research on this topic. Please do not sign your name to this survey.

Section 1

This section relates to how you view client relationship and culture issues within the organization. Please indicate your degree of agreement with the following statements by placing an X in the blank preceding the appropriate response.

strongly disagree	disagree	neutral	agree	strongly agree
_____1	_____2	_____3	_____4	_____5

1. There is a process in place to communicate to the vendor any concerns and issues affecting the quality of service.

strongly disagree	disagree	neutral	agree	strongly agree
_____1	_____2	_____3	_____4	_____5

2. The vendor clearly understood the client's requirements of the assignment.

strongly disagree	disagree	neutral	agree	strongly agree
_____1	_____2	_____3	_____4	_____5

3. The client requirements were clearly expressed.

strongly disagree	disagree	neutral	agree	strongly agree
_____1	_____2	_____3	_____4	_____5

4. Where you confident that the vendor made all reasonable efforts to understand your requirements?

strongly disagree	disagree	neutral	agree	strongly agree
_____1	_____2	_____3	_____4	_____5

5. The client took the time to explain the requirements fully.

strongly disagree	disagree	neutral	agree	strongly agree
_____1	_____2	_____3	_____4	_____5

6. The vendor assigned adequate time and resources to ensure that the client's requirements were fully understood.

strongly disagree	disagree	neutral	agree	strongly agree
_____1	_____2	_____3	_____4	_____5

7. The client understood the nature and limitations of the vendor services.

strongly disagree	disagree	neutral	agree	strongly agree
_____1	_____2	_____3	_____4	_____5

8. The vendor understood how outsourcing fit into the internal processes of the organization.

strongly disagree	disagree	neutral	agree	strongly agree
_____1	_____2	_____3	_____4	_____5

9. In your opinion are there significant differences in the political environments of the client and vendor respectively?

strongly disagree	disagree	neutral	agree	strongly agree
_____1	_____2	_____3	_____4	_____5

10. In your opinion are there significant differences in the cultures of the client and vendor respectively?

strongly disagree	disagree	neutral	agree	strongly agree
_____1	_____2	_____3	_____4	_____5

11. Outsourcing is a valuable resource to the client.

strongly disagree	disagree	neutral	agree	strongly agree
_____1	_____2	_____3	_____4	_____5

12. I am not aware of an effective process in place to communicate to vendor any concerns and issues affecting the quality of service.

strongly disagree	disagree	neutral	agree	strongly agree
_____1	_____2	_____3	_____4	_____5

13. I am not aware of an effective process in place to communicate to client any concern and issues affecting the quality of service.

strongly disagree	disagree	neutral	agree	strongly agree
_____1	_____2	_____3	_____4	_____5

14. There is a process in place to assess client's level of satisfaction.

strongly disagree	disagree	neutral	agree	strongly agree
_____1	_____2	_____3	_____4	_____5

15. There is a process in place to measure vendor's level of service.

strongly disagree	disagree	neutral	agree	strongly agree
_____1	_____2	_____3	_____4	_____5

Comments_____

_____

_____

_____

Section 2

This section rates your perception of the client service. Please indicate your degree of agreement with the following statements.

1. Majority of the time the clients requirements are reasonable.

strongly disagree	disagree	neutral	agree	strongly agree
_____1	_____2	_____3	_____4	_____5

2. Client's productivity has increased as a result as outsourcing.

strongly disagree	disagree	neutral	agree	strongly agree
_____1	_____2	_____3	_____4	_____5

3.Differences in the respective cultures of client and vendor may contribute to success or failure of projects.

strongly disagree	disagree	neutral	agree	strongly agree
_____1	_____2	_____3	_____4	_____5

4. Majority of the time results meet expectations of the client

strongly disagree	disagree	neutral	agree	strongly agree
_____1	_____2	_____3	_____4	_____5

5. Majority of the time tasks or project assignment is generally performed successfully by vendor.

strongly disagree	disagree	neutral	agree	strongly agree
_____1	_____2	_____3	_____4	_____5

Comments_____

_____

_____

_____

_____

Section 3

Open-Ended Questions

This section relates to the self-perception of the vendor. It is hope that these responses will benefit the organization.

1. Please identify any other factors not covered in this survey that you feel would cause the client to not renegotiate a contract. _____

_____

_____

_____

2. Please identify any other factors not covered in this survey that you feel would cause the vendor to not renegotiate a contract. _____

_____

_____

_____

3. Under what circumstances that have not been mentioned in this survey would you be more inclined to renegotiate a contract? _____

_____

_____

_____

Notes

Notes

Notes

Notes

www.ingramcontent.com/pod-product-compliance
Lightning Source LLC
La Vergne TN
LVHW042137040326
832903LV00011B/289/J